The Red Parrot and Other Stories

How this collection works

This *Read with Biff, Chip & Kipper* collection is the fourth in the series at Level 1. It is divided into two distinct halves.

The first half focuses on phonics-based reading practice. It contains eight amusing *Talk-about Situations* and a story called *The Red Parrot.* The second half contains four separate *Stories for Wider Reading* that use everyday language. These stories help to broaden your child's wider reading experience. There are fun activities to enjoy throughout the book.

How to use this book

Find a time to read with your child when they are not too tired and are happy to concentrate for about ten minutes. Reading at this stage should be a shared and enjoyable experience. It is best to choose just the *Talk-about Situations* or one of the stories for each session.

There are tips for reading together for each part of the book. The first tips are on pages 6 and 28. They show you how to introduce your child to the phonics stories. Tips to tell you how you can best approach reading the stories with a wider vocabulary are given on page 50.

Enjoy sharing the stories!

The **Helping Your Child to Read** handbook contains a wealth of practical information, tips and activities.

OXFORD
UNIVERSITY PRESS

Oxford University Press is a department of the University of Oxford.
It furthers the University's objective of excellence in research, scholarship,
and education by publishing worldwide. Oxford is a registered trade mark
of Oxford University Press in the UK and in certain other countries

Talk-about Situations, The Red Parrot first published in 2016
Can You See Me? first published in 2003
The Headache, Who Did That?, The Pet Shop first published in 1995

ISBN: 978-0-19-274474-6

10 9 8 7 6 5 4 3 2 1

Paper used in the production of this book is a natural, recyclable product made
from wood grown in sustainable forests. The manufacturing process conforms
to the environmental regulations of the country of origin.

Printed in China

Acknowledgements

Series Editor: Annemarie Young

The Red Parrot

and Other Stories

Phonics

Stories for Wider Reading

OXFORD
UNIVERSITY PRESS

Tips for the Talk-about Situations

These eight amusing situations are designed to motivate your child to predict what might happen next.

- Tell your child they are going to look at a series of pictures where something is about to happen.
- Talk about what is in the picture. Ask your child what is happening and what they think is going to happen next. Ask them to read any sound effect words in the picture, for example 'Rat-a-tat-tat!'.
- When you turn the page to see what actually happens, the outcome may or may not be what you expect! Talk about it.
- Ask your child to read the sound effect words in the picture (for example, 'Bam!'), and to read the simple sentence under the picture. All of the words on the outcome pages are phonically decodable.

Have fun!

Find the ten bugs hidden in the pictures.

The talk-about situations practise these letter sounds:

a   i   o   u   e   b   d   f   h   k
l   m   p   r   t   ss   ff   ll   ck

For more hints and tips on helping your child become a successful and enthusiastic reader look at our website www.oxfordowl.co.uk.

Talk-about Situations

Let's have some fun.

Talk about each picture.

Guess what's going to happen next!

What is Kipper doing?
What will happen next?

Kipper fell in the mud!

What are Mum and Dad doing?
What will happen next?

Mum fell. Dad fell off!

What will happen next?

13

The cat did not run!

What is Kipper doing?
What is Floppy doing?
What will happen next?

15

Kipper let go of the lid.

Tick-tock!

What is in the oven?
What is Dad going to do?

Bad luck, Dad!

What is making that noise?

It can tap and peck!

Rat-a-tat-tat!

Happy Birthday Mum!

What's in the box?

Mum got a kiss!

What is Kipper doing?
What will happen next?

A rip in the rabbit!

Matching

Match the words to the pictures.

Tick-tock!

Uck!

Bam!

Hiss!

Tap! Tap! Tap!

Maze

Follow Mum and Dad through the maze in the pram race.

FINISH

Read these sentences again

Kipper fell in the mud!

Bad luck, Dad!

Mum fell. Dad fell off!

It can tap and peck!

The cat did not run!

Mum got a kiss!

Kipper let go of the lid.

A rip in the rabbit!

27

Tips for Reading *The Red Parrot*

- Talk about the title and the picture on the opposite page.
- Find the letters *R* and *rr* in the title and talk about the sound they make when you read them.
- Look at the words on page 30. Say the sounds in each word and then say the word (e.g. *r-e-d*, *red*; *b-u-ck-e-t*, *bucket*).
- The story uses the word *went* on page 38. This is a 'tricky' word at this stage. Read it to your child.
- Read the story with your child, placing your finger under each word as you read together.
- Read the story again and encourage your child to do most of the reading.
- Give lots of praise as your child reads with you.
- Do the fun activities at the end of the story.

Children enjoy re-reading stories and this helps to build their confidence.

Have fun!

 After you have read the story, find the single feather hidden in every picture.

The main sounds practised in this story are 'r' as in *red*, *parrot* and *rock*, 'ck' as in *rock*, *back* and *bucket*, and 'f' as in *fun*, *fell* and *fed*.

 For more hints and tips on helping your child become a successful and enthusiastic reader look at our website www.oxfordowl.co.uk.

The Red Parrot

Read these words

red	pa**rr**ot
ran	**r**o**ck**
bu**ck**et	ba**ck**
fun	**f**ell
fed	**c**ap

Biff had a red parrot cap.

The parrot sat on a bucket.

Biff got a net.

Biff ran to get the parrot.

The parrot sat on a rock.

The parrot sat on a cat.

The cat got mad!

The parrot went back to
the rock.

The cat ran to the rock.

The cat got a nip!

Biff ran to the cat.

The parrot had fun.

It got a nut.

The nut fell on Biff.

Biff fed the parrot.

The parrot sat on Biff!

Where did the parrot go?

Which of these things did the parrot sit on?

Choose one of the words to finish the sentence.

The parrot sat on a _____.

Spot the pair

Which two parrot caps are identical?

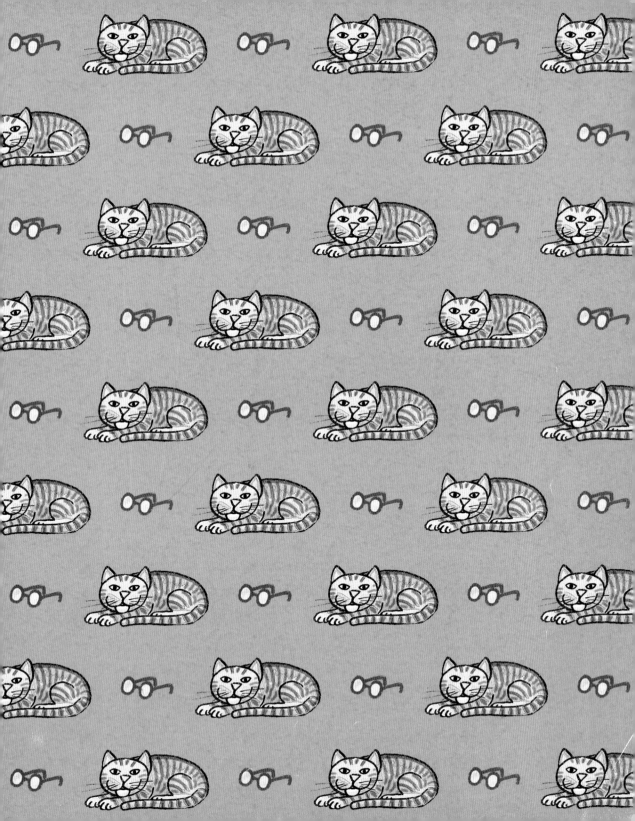

Stories for Wider Reading

Tips for Reading Together

These four stories use simple everyday language. Some of the words used are not decodable, but you can help your child to read them in the context of the story. For example, ask them to guess the name of each instrument in *The Headache* by looking at the picture before reading the text, or to tell you what the animals are in *The Pet Shop* as you read the story together.

- For each story, talk about the title and look through the pictures so that your child can see what each one is about.
- Read the story to your child, placing your finger under each word as you read.
- Read the story again and encourage your child to join in.
- Give lots of praise as your child reads with you.
- Talk about the story and do the fun activities at the end of each story.

Have fun!

After you have read *Can You See Me?* find the green frog hidden in every picture.

These stories include these common words: all   children
me   my   oh   no!   they   wanted   was   who   you

For more hints and tips on helping your child become a successful and enthusiastic reader look at our website www.oxfordowl.co.uk.

Can You See Me?

Can you see my ted?

Can you see my dog?

Can you see my big, red frog?

Can you see my tiger?

Is it in the tree?

Can you see me?

Talk about the story

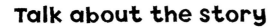

Where did you see Biff hiding?

How many toys can you see
in Kipper's bedroom?

What other animals has
Kipper painted?

What are your
favourite toys?

Odd one out

Which is the odd one out? Say why.

The Headache

Dad had a trumpet.

Chip had a drum.

Biff had a recorder.

Kipper had a guitar.

Mum had a headache!

Talk about the story

What are the four instruments in the story?

Which one did Kipper have?

Why did Mum have a headache?

What instrument would you like to play? Why?

Odd one out

What are these instruments? Which one is not in the story?

Answer: trumpet, recorder, guitar, harp, drum. The harp is not in the story.

Who Did That?

Mum was cross.

"Who did that?" she said.

"It was Chip," said Biff.

"It was Kipper," said Chip.

"It was Floppy," said Kipper.

"It was Floppy," said Biff.

"It was not Floppy," said Dad.

"It was me!"

Talk about the story

Why was Mum cross?

Who did Kipper blame?

What did Dad say?

Have you ever made a mess? What was it? Did you clean it up?

Spot the difference

Find the five differences in the two pictures.

The Pet Shop

The children wanted a pet.

Chip wanted a rat.

"Oh no!" said Kipper.

Biff wanted a spider.

"Oh no!" said Mum.

Kipper wanted a snake.

"Oh no!" said Chip.

They all wanted a goldfish!

Talk about the story

What pet did Chip want?

Who said no to the snake?

Why do you think they all wanted a goldfish?

What sort of pet would you like?

Spot the pair

Find the two identical snakes.

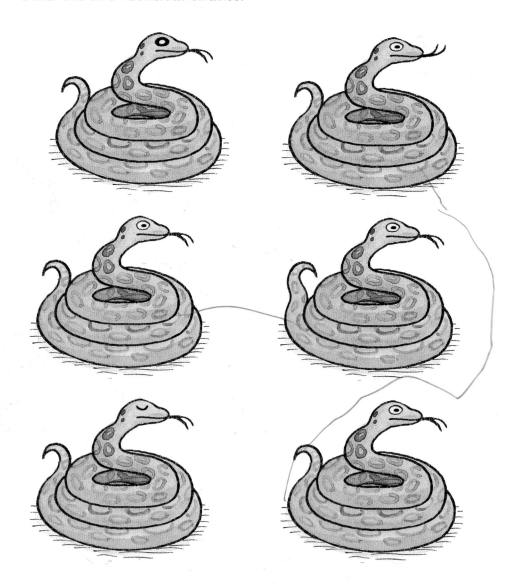

Answer: left middle and bottom right

Tangled lines

Who wanted which pet?

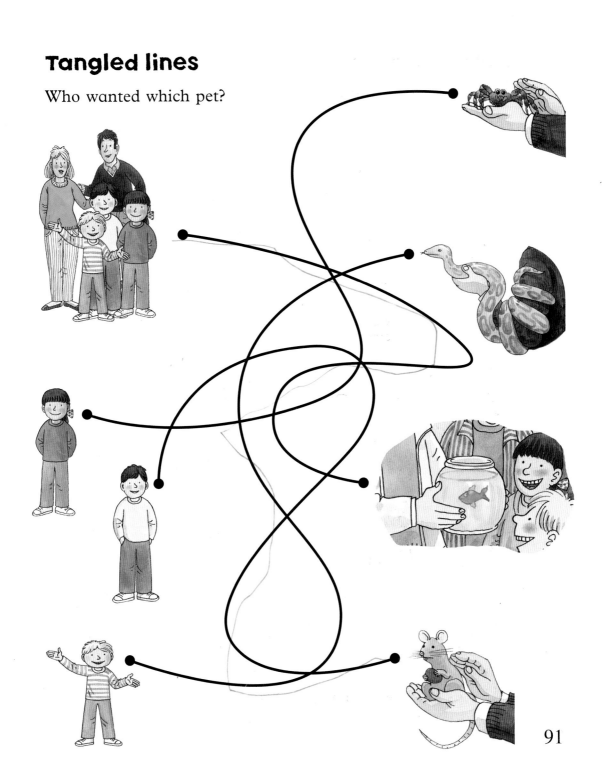

Rhyming pairs

Find the rhyming pairs.

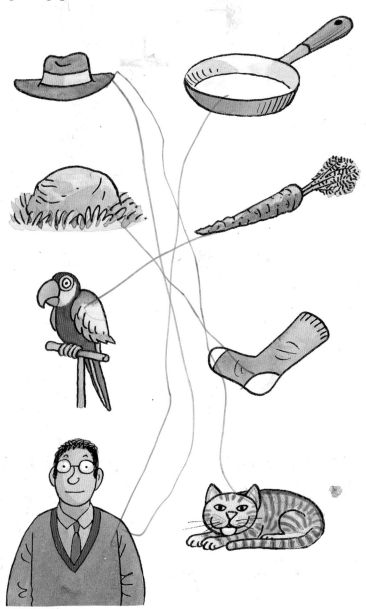

Phonics support

READ WITH Biff, Chip & Kipper

Flashcards are a really fun way to practise phonics and build reading skills. **Age 3+**

My Phonics Kit is designed to support you and your child as you practise phonics together at home. It includes stickers, workbooks, interactive eBooks, support for parents and more! **Age 5+**

Read Write Inc. Phonics: A range of fun rhyming stories to support decoding skills. **Age 4+**

Songbirds Phonics: Lively and engaging phonics stories from former Children's Laureate, Julia Donaldson. **Age 4+**